ARIZONA
Pathways

TRAILS OF HISTORY

ARIZONA
HIGHWAYS BOOK

Text by James E. Cook

Photography by *Arizona Highways* Contributors

Edited by Dean Smith

Cartography by Don Bufkin

Illustrations by Bill Ahrendt

(COVER BACKGROUND PHOTOGRAPH) *Dawn breaks over construction of "The Stack" near the junction of Interstate Highways 10 and 17 in Phoenix.* CHRISTINE KEITH (INSETS, LEFT TO RIGHT) *Staging a reenactment, modern pioneers travel the Honeymoon Trail by covered wagon.* VAL STANNARD *Spring flowers fill a desert roadway near the old Gila Trail east of Yuma.* JAMES TALLON *General Phillip St. George Cooke who led the Mormon Battalion and built a wagon road across southern Arizona.* ARIZONA HISTORICAL SOCIETY

(PRECEDING PAGE) *Cavalry troops ride out of Fort Bowie, in southeastern Arizona. The troops protected immigrants traveling through Apache Pass along the Gila Trail.* NATIONAL ARCHIVES

Table of Contents

VAL STANNARD

MANLEY-PRIM PHOTOGRAPHY

JACK DYKINGA

Arizona Pathways - Trails of History

Hugh Harelson - Publisher / Wesley Holden - Managing Editor / Robert J. Farrell - Associate Editor
Lynne Hamilton - Art Director / James R. Metcalf - Design & Production

Prepared by the Related Products Section of *Arizona Highways* magazine, a monthly publication of the Arizona Department of Transportation.

Library of Congress Catalog Number 89-80695 softcover / 89-80751 hardcover
ISBN 0-916179-25-7 softcover / ISBN 0-916179-26-5 hardcover

Published in the interest of young people
to improve their knowledge of early Arizona immigration.

ARIZONA HISTORICAL SOCIETY

UNIVERSITY OF NEW MEXICO PRESS

VAL STANNARD

JERRY SIEVE

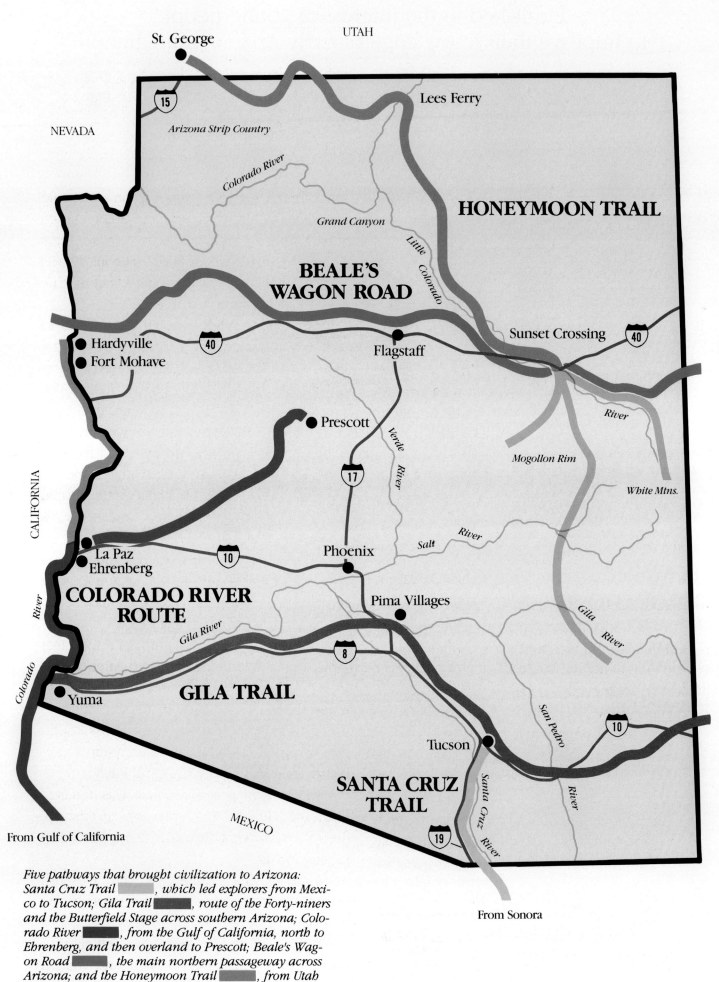

St. George

UTAH

NEVADA

HONEYMOON TRAIL

Lees Ferry

Arizona Strip Country

Colorado River

Grand Canyon

Little Colorado

BEALE'S WAGON ROAD

Sunset Crossing

Hardyville
Fort Mohave

Flagstaff

NEW MEXICO

River

Prescott

Mogollon Rim

White Mtns.

Verde River

CALIFORNIA

Salt

River

La Paz
Ehrenberg

Phoenix

COLORADO RIVER ROUTE

Pima Villages

Gila River

Gila River

Gila River

GILA TRAIL

Yuma

San Pedro River

Tucson

SANTA CRUZ TRAIL

Santa Cruz River

MEXICO

From Gulf of California

From Sonora

Five pathways that brought civilization to Arizona: Santa Cruz Trail ▢, which led explorers from Mexico to Tucson; Gila Trail ▢, route of the Forty-niners and the Butterfield Stage across southern Arizona; Colorado River ▢, from the Gulf of California, north to Ehrenberg, and then overland to Prescott; Beale's Wagon Road ▢, the main northern passageway across Arizona; and the Honeymoon Trail ▢, from Utah to northern and eastern Arizona.

OLD ROADS TELL THEIR STORIES

A fragment of an old road hangs on an Arizona hillside like a poster on a wall. It fades in and out of the land without a beginning or an end. On some roads, the iron tires of ox-drawn wagons wore grooves into the ground, and even into the rocks. Driving past on a modern, paved highway, you wonder, where did that rugged old road go?

In a wetter, greener state, weeds would have covered up the old roads long ago. Then people wouldn't come across them and wonder whether the ruts were worn by stagecoaches or by the mule-drawn wagons of a frontier army on the move.

In Arizona's dry air, the tracks endure, teasing you with the stories the old roads could tell. Even in the forests of northern Arizona,

(ABOVE) *Carrying their families and possessions in small wagons, pioneers followed the pathways blazed by early explorers of the Arizona Territory.* VAL STANNARD

you can still see trails through the trees, and sometimes a "blaze" where a scout cut a patch of bark from a ponderosa pine to show others where the road went. Soon wagon wheels wore troughs in the ground that a mat of pine needles cannot hide.

Was it a long road, carrying adventurers to California to look for gold in 1849? Or was it a short road that led to someone's silver mine, and to a boom town that quickly faded? The old road you see may be going the same place you are. Often, the new road just moved over and found a more comfortable spot.

It occurred to us that some of these roads could tell how Arizona came to be, and what it is today. The five Arizona pathways we have chosen include:

• An ancient trail that carried Spanish and Mexican settlers north to Tucson.

• A road across southern Arizona that was used by Forty-niners going to California during the Gold Rush.

• Arizona's biggest river that was traveled from the Gulf of California by steamboats, then the trail went inland to Army forts and mining towns.

• A route that camels helped establish across northern Arizona; it later became one of America's best-known highways.

• The Honeymoon Trail that settlers followed from Utah into northern and eastern Arizona.

Geographic Contrasts

Geography and history help shape each other. Both hinge on transportation, how and why people went from place to place. Since about two-thirds of the people who live in the state were born somewhere else, our five pathways brought many of us to Arizona.

Distances are great in Arizona, which is 392 miles long and 338 miles across at its widest point. It is as big as several other states combined: Indiana, Ohio, West Virginia, Massachusetts, and Delaware. And you can throw in Rhode Island, which would fit inside our smallest county.

Deserts

There is hardly a state with more varied, jumbled terrain. Arizona is relatively flat across the deserts that cover the southwestern one-third of the state, making travel fairly rapid. But water was scarce and the distances were long, especially along the Gila Trail, the road many of the Forty-niners took to California.

Arizona's climate, notorious or glorious depending on whom you ask, is an important element of the state's geography. Humorists tell of the frontier soldier at Yuma who died and went to hell. He found that place chilly by comparison, and soon sent back for his blankets.

Yet in winter, the relatively warm desert makes Arizona a good place to live. The differences in altitude make for great differences in temperatures. While some desert towns in western Arizona frequently report the warmest summertime temperatures in the United States, it is not unheard of for a weather station in Arizona's high mountains to report the nation's coldest winter temperature.

Mountains

Hardly any place in the state is out of sight of mountains—sharp desert mountains that

stand against the sky like stage scenery, or forested, alpine mountains. The land rises more than two vertical miles between the lowest point in Arizona, 70 feet above sea level, south of Yuma, and the highest, 12,643 feet atop the San Francisco Peaks, north of Flagstaff. If Arizona were pressed out flat, it might be as big as Texas.

A rugged band of mountains lies diagonally across the center of Arizona, slanting from southeast to northwest. The northeastern part of the state is a plateau, with its own volcanic mountains and spectacular river canyons. The largest ponderosa pine forest in the world covers the south edge of this plateau, and slips over into the central uplands.

Giant saguaros, Arizona's most famous cacti, raise their arms at sunset on the southern Arizona desert. Unlike the popular concept of a Sahara landscape, this desert teems with fascinating plants, animals, and birds.
JACK DYKINGA

Raging rivers in flood season presented formidable barriers to Arizona newcomers in earlier days. The Little Colorado River, shown cascading over Grand Falls in northern Arizona, challenged travelers on the Honeymoon Trail from Utah. DICK DIETRICH

Rivers

While mountains had a lot to do with where the roads went, so did rivers. The run-ning waters had already found the path of least resistance across the land, often carving their way through the mountain barriers. Travelers needed the water in the rivers for themselves and for their oxen, mules, and horses. Grass near the rivers helped feed the livestock. Wild animals that came there for water helped feed the travelers. In the deserts of southwestern Arizona and the high plains of the northeast, the only wood for cooking fires might be found in groves along washes and rivers.

The wagons the travelers drove had iron tires, bands of metal bonded to wooden wheels. In the dry air of Arizona, the wooden spokes and rims, called fellies, shrank away from the tires. If a tire came loose, it could strand travelers many miles from a town, a fort, or a blacksmith. When a driver got a chance, he backed his wagon into a pool of water and let the wooden wheels soak up moisture. The wood expanded and kept the tires fitting tightly.

But rivers could also act as barriers. The Colorado River and some of its chief tributaries carved deep canyons, including the Grand Canyon, which posed awesome obstacles to settlers moving south from Utah on the Honeymoon Trail. How they got across the river is a brave, romantic part of Arizona history.

Early Roads

Pioneers didn't have many road-building tools, so early roads followed the easiest routes. A pathway might wander one way in a dry time of year, another during the rainy season, avoiding muddy places.

As more pioneers came, and more tools became available, a road might settle for a while in one place. When road builders figured out a way to cut through a hill or bridge a stream, the road became shorter. The Gila Trail, also known as the Butterfield Stage Trail, is a perfect example. Its route across Arizona was 437 miles long, but modern highways have shortened the trip to 372 miles. Finally, modern engineers fixed the roads in place with concrete or asphalt. And still, they find ways to make highways shorter.

Beale's Road, first traveled by camels in 1857, became today's Interstate Route 40, a multi-lane, divided freeway across the northern part of the state from New Mexico to California. If you look closely on either side of the freeway, you can trace three or four stages of that road. Weeds grow through some of the old abandoned stretches of pavement put down 60 years ago. You can let your imagination tell the story of Americans who followed their dreams down that road to California when cars were square and simple and slow.

That old pavement was replaced by newer, faster stretches; and they, in turn, were replaced by freeways. Some intermediate stretches are still used as local roads, going to farms and ranches and nearly abandoned towns.

Where have you been, old road? We wonder. The road invites us to come and see. □

Arizona Facts

- Arizona is divided into 15 counties. The largest, Coconino, is bigger than Vermont and Massachusetts combined.
- The highest temperature ever recorded in Arizona was 127 degrees (Fahrenheit) at Fort Mohave in 1896 and Parker in 1905.
- The lowest temperature on record was 40 degrees below zero at Hawley Lake in 1971.
- Arizona's northeast corner is at Four Corners, the only place where four states meet: Arizona, Utah, Colorado, and New Mexico.
- Arizona's major industries are service (which includes serving each other and tourists); trade and commerce; manufacturing; finance, insurance, and real estate; construction; mining; and government.
- There are 20 Indian reservations in Arizona.
- Arizona has 21 national parks, monuments, and other sites protected by the National Park Service; six national forests; and 25 state parks.

Chapter 1

SANTA CRUZ TRAIL

On a rainy day in March, 1856, a few dozen Mexicans sadly prepared to leave the village of Tucson. Some of their families had lived there for generations. The village was founded as a Spanish outpost in 1775, the same year the American Revolution began in New England. In 1854, however, Mexican President Antonio Lopez de Santa Anna had sold southern Arizona to the United States for 10 million dollars.

In the narrow streets of Tucson, outside the low-walled adobe houses, civilians and soldiers packed their belongings on mules and in crude wagons. This day was a turning point in their lives, and in the history of the American Southwest.

(LEFT) *First Coronado in 1540, and then other Spanish commanders in later centuries, led troops into Arizona, as in this reenactment at Tubac. The first Spanish presidio, or fort, was established at Tubac in 1752 and the second was at Tucson in 1775.* MANLEY-PRIM PHOTOGRAPHY

(ABOVE) *Elephant Head, a spectacular rock formation in the Santa Rita Mountains, is a famous landmark along the Santa Cruz Trail.* JACK DYKINGA

Seventeen boisterous Americans could hardly wait for the Mexicans to leave. U.S. soldiers had not yet arrived to occupy the territory, but the United States had owned it for more than a year and a half. The Americans patched together a flag pole of mesquite branches. Despite the objections of the Mexican commander of Tucson, the Americans raised the flag of the United States over the plaza in the walled village.

Well-traveled valley

When the Mexicans straggled south out of Tucson, rain muffling the creaking of wagons and pack saddles, they were traveling a trail that followed the course of the Santa Cruz River, one of the earliest pathways into Arizona. That route is still an important pathway-- Interstate Route 19, a 63-mile freeway connecting Tucson with Mexico.

Let's take a look at this natural pathway and try to recapture what it was like for travelers of past centuries. The Santa Cruz River begins in Arizona, southeast of Tucson. It swings southward into Mexico, then arcs west and north to cross the border again, east of Nogales, and goes northward 182 miles to join the Gila River.

The pretty valley of the Santa Cruz is a narrow, curving band of green along the river. It enters Arizona from Mexico at an elevation of

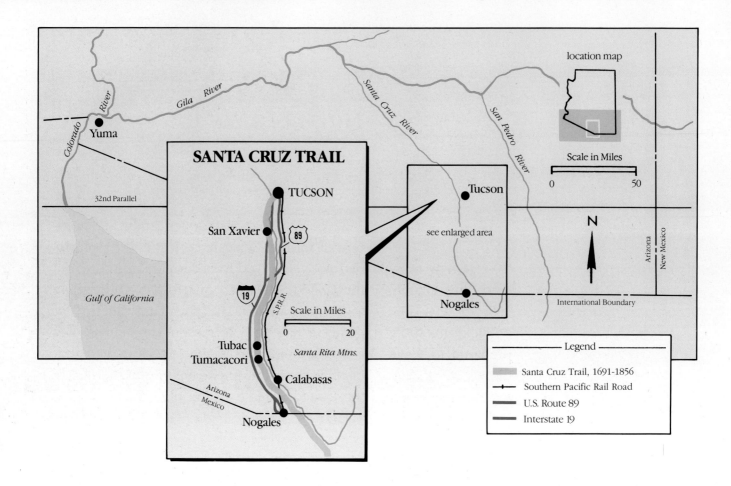

SANTA CRUZ TRAIL

Legend
- Santa Cruz Trail, 1691-1856
- Southern Pacific Rail Road
- U.S. Route 89
- Interstate 19

3,865 feet and meanders downhill and northward to Tucson at 2,389 feet elevation. Ancient Indians had used the old valley trail for a trade route; then came the Spaniards and Mexicans who used the same route for approximately 300 years.

Spaniards first explored the area in the 1500s. Late in the 1600s, they used this corridor to establish Roman Catholic missions to the Indians on the northern frontier of New Spain. The Spanish also established isolated ranches and mines. To protect settlers from Indian raids, they founded two presidios, or fortified military outposts: Tubac in 1752, and Tucson in 1775.

The pathway runs north from the border with Mexico, beginning at the pass through wooded hills where the twin cities of Nogales, Arizona, and Nogales, Sonora have grown. Nogales is Spanish for "walnuts," and the cities were named for the walnut trees that grow there. Among Arizona's wide weather extremes, Nogales is a pleasant middle ground: relatively cool summers with monsoon rains,

and mild winters with only occasional snows. American Nogales has a population of about 17,000. The population of Nogales, Sonora, is estimated at more than 225,000. The larger Mexican population, typical of border cities today, is supported partly by several American-owned factories in the Sonoran city. Nogales is a popular destination for American tourists. It also is the gateway to the coastal highway route to Mexico City.

Traveling north beside the belt of greenery along the Santa Cruz River, the settlers and soldiers followed a rutted path that hardly resembled a road. They had few wagons, so most goods were transported by mule train.

Among the willows and low mesquite trees, travelers replenished their food supply with jackrabbits or an occasional deer. There were no roadside restaurants or stores, of course, and the pioneers cooked over open campfires.

They had to be careful not to wander too far from camp, even in search of food, because Apache Indians were a constant threat.

Pete Kitchen, one of the most colorful of the early American pioneers, operated this ranch north of Nogales in the early 1860s and defended his home against fierce Apache attacks long after other ranchers were driven out. ARIZONA HISTORICAL SOCIETY

Instead of turning an automobile ignition key, the Hispanic pioneers had to feed and harness their mules, then hitch them to wagons or load them with pack saddles. The animals were not always cooperative.

When everything was ready for the day's trip, the travelers took to a trail that was sometimes only a worn place through the grass and brush, close to the river in dry weather, a bit farther out when it was wet.

A Desert River

The Santa Cruz River is usually dry for long periods of time, but seasonal rains make it flow, and even flood. Then it simply gets wider, rather than cutting a deep channel. People who live in wetter climates expect a river to flow year-round. But several Arizona rivers simply disappear into the sand, and others have been dammed upstream to store water and control flooding.

Humorists have a lot of fun with the image of first-time Arizona visitors driving across bridges that have no water beneath them. They tell of an Arizona native who visited upstate New York. When he returned, a friend

The modern community of Rio Rico nestles at the foot of the Cayetano Mountains north of Nogales. Here the Santa Cruz River winds through vistas of quiet grandeur. RANDY PRENTICE

asked what he thought of the deep, wide Hudson River.

"Well, it's hard to say," the Arizonan answered. "It was full of water the whole time I was there."

Calabasas

Even in territorial days, the shallow surface waters of the Santa Cruz River seldom flowed above ground past the old village of Calabasas, a few miles north of the Mexican border. Spanish priests built a mission at Calabasas in the 1700s. The village was later a center for Mexican farms and ranches. Raiding Apaches frequently forced settlers to abandon it.

The conflict between Europeans and Indians began when the first Spaniards came into this area in 1539, and continued through 1886. It was more than a turf war. Indians felt they belonged to the land and must live in harmony with it, taking only what they needed. Europeans, however, felt the land belonged to them, to own, survey, exploit, and sell. The difference in views is so fundamental that even today the two races sometimes have trouble understanding each other.

Spain used Tubac and Tucson to stage occasional raids against the Apaches, but rarely had the manpower or supplies to defend its northern frontier adequately. After Mexico ejected the Spanish in a revolution that ended in 1821, the new nation had even fewer resources for its remotest provinces.

Where Calabasas stood, the modern planned community of Rio Rico has grown up. It is home for retirees and some people who work in busy Nogales. Its resort attracts

visitors drawn by the green valley and its border of tall mountains.

The Santa Cruz valley separates two kinds of terrain. To the west, low mountains screen the valley from the harsh Sonoran Desert. On the east, the forested Santa Rita Mountains rise 6,000 feet above the river, and more than 9,000 feet above sea level.

Southern Arizona has several abrupt mountains or small ranges called "sky islands," because they are not connected to any other mountains. The steep mountainsides start out covered with desert brush, but their tops are crowned with pine forests. Each "sky island" is a separate segment of the Coronado National Forest.

Arizona's first sawmill was built in the Santa Ritas in 1857, but that was after the United States owned the area. Hispanic settlers had very little lumber, and built their homes of adobe and their furniture from rough wood and leather.

Tumacacori

A few miles north of Rio Rico is Tumacacori National Monument, the partially restored ruins of a mission church built on the west bank of the Santa Cruz River about 1800. Earlier, Father Eusebio Francisco Kino founded the first Tumacacori Mission at an Indian village on the east side of the river. Kino, a Jesuit priest, introduced Christianity to the Indians in 1691. He also taught them cattle ranching, which has been a major industry in the area ever since.

Tubac

The first European settlement in Arizona was Tubac, 10 miles north of Tumacacori, established by the Spanish in 1752. Captain Juan Bautista de Anza used Tubac to rest and reprovision a large expedition that began a historic journey to California in 1775. Members of his expedition founded San Francisco.

In addition to serving as a center for cattle ranching and farming, Tubac was headquarters for some of the earliest mines in the area. Arizona's first newspaper, *The Weekly Arizonian*, was published at Tubac in 1859.

Articles in that newspaper ignited the first recorded duel in Arizona. When editor Edward Cross criticized mine owner Sylvester Mowry for promoting the creation of Arizona Territory, Mowry challenged him to duel with rifles. Neither man hit the other. Mowry fired his final shot into the air to avoid killing Cross, and they retired from the field to toast each other's survival.

Tubac is quieter now, a community whose residents work to preserve its scenic setting and its heritage. Its architecture imitates that of colonial times. Tubac State Historic Park preserves the hand press on which *The Weekly Arizonian* was printed.

As you travel northward from Tubac toward Tucson, the plain of the Santa Cruz broadens. You pass Green Valley, an aptly-named community founded in the 1960s. In a state where towns once grew haphazardly, several planned communities such as Rio Rico and Green Valley have emerged since World War II. Green Valley has one area for retirees and another for families who simply want a home in a scenic setting.

A few miles farther north is one of the Southwest's most beautiful missions: San Xavier del Bac, "the white dove of the desert." Father Kino first came to this Tohono O'odham (Papago) village before 1700. The graceful design of the present mission church was finished nearly a century later.

Tucson

At the northern end of the Santa Cruz Trail is Tucson, founded by Spanish Colonel Don Hugo Oconor and Father Francisco Garces. It has grown from a humble cluster of adobe dwellings to Arizona's second-largest metropolitan center.

Tucson once looked more like an Indian pueblo than a European or American town. Settlers lived on what they could grow on small farms and ranches outside the presidio's

adobe walls. They adapted to the frontier by thinking and dressing more like Native Americans than like Hispanics in the larger cities to the south.

Now more than 600,000 people live in the Tucson metropolitan area. Few American cities have such a scenic setting, ringed by desert mountains. On the east and west sides of the city, two sections of Saguaro National Monument contain majestic forests of the tall

Text continued on page 20

(ABOVE) *Indians of the Santa Cruz valley and colonists from Mexico worshipped in the Tumacacori Mission church near Tubac nearly two centuries ago. Today, partially restored and resplendent in its floral setting, Tumacacori is a mecca for tourists.* JACK DYKINGA

(FOLLOWING PANEL, PAGES 18 AND 19) *The arrival of a Spanish military unit at the Tubac presidio in the early 1750s. Spanish soldiers and priests originally established Tubac as a presidio, or fortress in the Santa Cruz River Valley. From there the priests converted the Indians of the area to Christianity, and the soldiers searched the surrounding country for precious minerals, establishing several rich silver mines.*

In Arizona's most famous duel, Edward Cross and Sylvester Mowry met outside Tubac in 1859 to defend their honor with rifles. Neither man could hit the other, so they retired to toast their survival.

Text continued from page 17

saguaro cactus, the traditional symbol of Arizona and the Southwest.

After the United States acquired southern Arizona in the Gadsden Purchase of 1854, Americans began to build their kind of town. They were joined by Mexicans, some returning to their hometown and some looking for new opportunities there. Together, they developed a rich and varied culture. Tucson became a commercial center for southern Arizona and northern Mexico.

It was the largest city in Arizona until around 1915, when Phoenix surpassed it. It was inevitable that Tucson become Americanized, but it has kept a strong flavor of Mexico in its architecture and social life. Its barrios, predominantly Hispanic neighborhoods, cling to their identities. Tucson has a pleasant climate—six to eight degrees cooler in the summertime than Phoenix—and that has made it a popular destination for vacationers.

There are copper mines nearby, large ranches, and military installations. Many Tucsonans work in modern high-tech factories. Astronomers like the view from southern Arizona's high peaks, and it is said that there are more telescopes within 50 miles of Tucson than anywhere else on earth.

By the time Mexican settlers moved out of Tucson in March of 1856, the Santa Cruz Trail was connected to the Gila Trail, a new United States route to the Pacific.

The Santa Cruz Trail began as an old Indian path that led Europeans into the land that would be called Arizona. The modern freeway version of the Santa Cruz Trail is still an important link between Mexico and the United States. □

(ABOVE) *Beautiful Mission San Xavier del Bac, built in the 1790s on the site of an earlier Father Kino mission, is one of the triumphs of Spanish colonial architecture. The Santa Catalina Mountains provide a scenic back-drop for the historic "white dove of the desert."*
WILLARD CLAY

(RIGHT) *In the 1890s, before its restoration, San Xavier showed the ravages of time and desert sandstorms.*
ARIZONA STATE LIBRARY AND ARCHIVES

21

- 1691: Father Eusebio Francisco Kino enters what will become Arizona.

- 1752: Tubac Presidio founded by the Spanish.

- 1775: Tucson Presidio founded by Oconor and Garces.

- 1821: Mexico wins independence from Spain. Four years later, the Erie Canal opens from New York to Pennsylvania.

- 1846-48: Mexican War yields northern two-thirds of Arizona to the United States. The Mormons begin their trek to Salt Lake City in 1846.

- 1854: Land south of Gila River acquired by the Gadsden Purchase, added to New Mexico Territory. Four years earlier, Henry Clay presented the Compromise of 1850.

- 1856: U.S. soldiers occupy southern Arizona, below the Gila River.

- 1863: Through the efforts of leaders at Tubac and Tucson, Arizona becomes a separate territory. Five years earlier, 1858, the Atlantic Cable was completed to link Europe and America.

(LEFT) *Modern metropolitan Tucson, a community of 600,000, is world-famous for its climate and its delightful blending of the cultures of Mexico and the United States. This business, educational, and industrial center of southern Arizona has a proud history dating back to 1775.* RANDY PRENTICE

(INSET) *Tucson's growth in recent decades is evident when we compare photographs of today's city and one from the 1890s, both taken from "A" Mountain.*
BANCROFT LIBRARY, UNIVERSITY OF CALIFORNIA, BERKELEY

Chapter 2

THE GILA TRAIL

The stagecoach jolted along the trail at an average four-and-a-half miles per hour, about as fast as a modern jogger moves. That meant it was four hours or more between stage stops. This stage was not the big, graceful Concord coach seen in movies but a more open wagon with a simple roof and hard wooden seats.

The ride was hot and dusty, unless it was cold and dusty. The passengers—a mine promoter, a gambler, a butcher, an Army wife following her husband west — hadn't bathed in days. Constant motion, and the bad food at the stage stations, made some of them ill.

Some smoked, some drank, some dipped snuff. An Army major traveling across Arizona on the Butterfield Route sized up his fellow travelers and said, "They did not make the most agreeable companions."

But never mind the hardships. They were going to California along the Gila Trail, and the Butterfield Stage was the fastest way to go.

Smooth, divided highways (Interstates 8 and 10) now cross the desert that the Gila Trail once traversed from New Mexico to California, curving like a bow across the map of southern Arizona. The trail originally ran along the banks of the Gila River, but in some places explorers found easier traveling away from the river a few miles. Although the route was relocated several times over the years and was known by different names, it still followed the same general path as the Gila River.

We're going to travel it the hard way, though. We'll walk parts of the Gila Trail, as mountain men and soldiers did. We're going to go in wagons, like Forty-niners rushing to the California gold fields. And we're going to ride the jolting, bouncing Butterfield Stage, the first reliable coach line to link East and West.

(LEFT) *The Gila River flows through several steep canyons in eastern Arizona, such as this one called the "Gila Box." Pioneers seeking a passage for their wagons to California found it necessary to leave the Gila valley and travel through the less rugged country to the south.* JACK DYKINGA

(ABOVE) *This southern portion of the Gila Trail snaked westward across the desert toward Tucson. The Butterfield Stage route passed this way near Bowie in what is now Cochise County.* MANLEY-PRIM PHOTOGRAPHY

Mountain Men

In 1825 and 1826, when the land we call Arizona belonged to Mexico, James Ohio Pattie trapped beaver along the length of the Gila, which he called the "Helay." Pattie told his

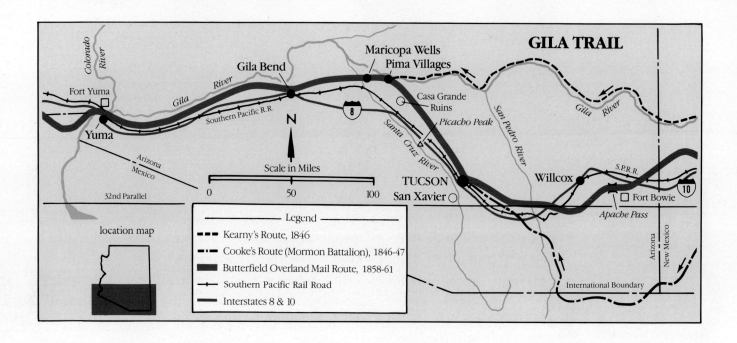

Legend
- - - Kearny's Route, 1846
- · - Cooke's Route (Mormon Battalion), 1846-47
▬▬▬ Butterfield Overland Mail Route, 1858-61
-+- Southern Pacific Rail Road
━━━ Interstates 8 & 10

location map

Scale in Miles
0   50   100

Butterfield Stage

story to a ghost writer, who wrote our earliest English language description of the Gila. And while the river has served as a pathway, a landmark, and an international boundary, it has never been much of a river: That is to say, it seldom carries much water. Pattie found the place where the Salt River empties into the Gila, southwest of today's Phoenix.

"It (the Salt) affords more water at this point than the Helay," he reported. The Salt River is still more important to Arizona, but not to the history of the West.

The rivers join near the center of Arizona. In several places east of there, the Gila flows through narrow mountain canyons. The U.S. Army's General Stephen Watts Kearny and his men found the canyons too rugged for wheeled vehicles when they struggled through them with two cannon in 1846 during the Mexican War. So a procession of soldiers and surveyors located the road which arcs to the south, connecting with the central portion of the Gila near Phoenix.

To follow the trail logically from east to west, as tens of thousands of pioneers did, we have to move back and forth in time, borrowing the best stories from their journals.

Let's begin in 1858. John Butterfield had a contract to carry the U.S. mail from St. Louis to San Francisco, and he put together a remarkable stagecoach line. He told his drivers, "Remember, boys, nothing on God's earth must stop the U.S. Mail," and nothing did.

The stage took from 23 to 26 days to cover 2,700 miles. For the first several days west of St. Louis, we might have ridden in one of the big Concord coaches. On the deserts of the Southwest, however, Butterfield switched to simpler wagons drawn by mules.

The land is high, arid grasslands west of Steins Pass, New Mexico, where today's Interstate Highway 10 enters Arizona. The plains are about 3,600 feet above sea level. This was important cattle ranching country in later years, after the frontier was a bit tamer.

Stage stations, 20 to 40 miles apart, were crude adobe buildings surrounded by low walls. The coach got fresh horses and drivers at these stations, and passengers could eat food that usually was unappetizing: beans, dried beef or salt pork, biscuits or cornbread.

Each station had four or five armed men to guard against Apache attack. Indians rarely attacked a coach, because passengers carried

few things the Apaches could use. But the stations were ideal places to raid for horses and supplies.

The station at Apache Pass, in southeastern Arizona, was especially dangerous and Butterfield asked the Army to build a fort there. Fort Bowie wasn't built until after the stagecoaches had stopped coming this way in 1861 (the Butterfield Route was moved northward at the beginning of the Civil War). But Fort Bowie protected later travelers, and today you can visit its ruins at a national historic site about 15 miles south of Interstate 10.

The stagecoach skirted the north end of the Chiricahua and Dragoon mountain ranges, stopping at San Pedro River station, near where the town of Benson is today. Here we have to drop back to 1846 to pick up a remarkable story.

(ABOVE) *In the 1890s Fort Bowie, in the far southeastern corner of Arizona, provided vital protection for hardy travelers on the Gila Trail.* ARIZONA HISTORICAL FOUNDATION.

(RIGHT) *Today the historic fort is a national monument. These crumbling adobe walls were once the busy barracks of cavalry troops.* JACK DYKINGA

Mormon Battalion

During the Mexican War, Captain Philip St. George Cooke and a few Regular Army officers and sergeants led 340 Mormons to California. The Mormons had volunteered to go as soldiers as a way of escaping persecution in the Midwest. While they were going, the government decided, they might as well build a wagon road.

Many years earlier, Spanish and Mexican ranchers had raised cattle along the San Pedro River. Apache raids had forced them to abandon their ranches, and the cattle had grown wild. A herd of these wild bulls attacked the Mormon Battalion, wrecking wagons and injuring men and mules. The bulls were hard to kill, and it took the escorting soldiers several hours to end the battle.

The battalion "captured" Tucson without opposition. Mexican soldiers pulled out of town until the battalion left, and civilians sold supplies to the Americans.

Fourteen years later, a passenger on the first westbound Butterfield Stage wrote:

"Tucson is a small place, consisting of a few adobe houses. The inhabitants are mainly Mexicans. There are but few Americans,

The Mormon Battalion engaged in only one battle during its 1846 march across southern Arizona. Wild bulls from an abandoned Spanish ranch attacked Capt. Philip St. George Cooke's soldiers just south of today's Benson and gored several men and mules. But this "Battle of the Bulls" did not stop these hardy men who pushed on to carve out the first wagon road to California.

though they keep the two or three stores, and are elected to the town offices. The Apaches are somewhat troublesome in the vicinity. [We had to] drive 40 miles to the next station in the Picacho Pass, before we came to desirable water."

Then as now, the trail went almost straight northwest out of Tucson. The highway goes through the irrigated farmlands of the Marana district, then into nearly flat desert, covered in spring by carpets of wildflowers.

Battle of Picacho Peak

Picacho Peak, a spire of stone along the Gila Trail, rises from the flat desert 40 miles northwest of Tucson. Newman Peak rises to the east, and between them is Picacho Pass, site of a Civil War skirmish in 1862.

The Confederacy had proclaimed its version of the territory of Arizona, and 65 Confederate soldiers occupied the area. But the Union's "California Column" was marching eastward. Patrols from the Union and Confederate forces clashed in Picacho Pass April 15, 1862. Three Californians were killed and three wounded. Two Confederates were wounded and three captured. The vastly outnumbered Confederates retreated to Tucson and then east to New Mexico.

From Picacho Peak, the Gila Trail continues through Pinal County and the Casa Grande Valley, a major farming area. The valley's biggest city, Casa Grande, takes its name ("Big House" in Spanish) from the nearby Casa Grande Ruins National Monument. The four-story structure was built by Hohokam Indians about A.D. 1300. Spanish explorers marveled at it, and James Ohio Pattie visited it in 1826.

Picacho Peak, which towers above the desert 40 miles northwest of Tucson, was the site of Arizona's only major Civil War skirmish. RANDY PRENTICE

Bumpy Travel

Not far west of Casa Grande were the scattered "Pima Villages," important to European travelers for several decades. Indian farmers provided food for the travelers and grain and fodder for their animals.

Most early travelers did not go as far north as the point where the Salt River joins the Gila River southwest of Phoenix. It's an important reference point, however. West of this junction, the Gila makes two 90-degree turns, going south and then west again, forming "The Great Bend Of The Gila" near the modern town of Gila Bend.

Most pioneers cut across this bend a few miles north of where Interstate 8 goes today. At Maricopa Wells, one Butterfield passenger wrote, "Here the water is very good." Every third or fourth station had a blacksmith and a wheelwright who could repair damaged coaches. Maricopa Wells was one such stop.

At Maricopa Wells, the "Forty-mile Desert" began. The trail to Gila River Station, where the town of Gila Bend stands today, was a waterless stretch, even in winter. On Decem-

ber 25, 1846, Miles Thompson, a private in the Mormon Battalion, wrote in his diary: "Christmas. Left the Pemoes [Pimas]. Traveled 20 miles and camped without water. Traveled through a sandy desert. Ate our Christmas supper by the roadside. Had cold beans, pancakes, and pumpkin sauce."

The Butterfield Stage was scheduled to reach the Gila River Station at 9 p.m. on a Wednesday; it would get to Yuma 30 hours later. One traveler described passengers enduring a crowded stagecoach at night: "Three in a row, actuated by the same instantaneous impulse, we would solemnly rise from our seats, bump our heads against the low roof, and, returning, vigorously ram the again rising seat we had incontinently left."

Despite the pounding, most travelers eventually drifted off to sleep, waking to find themselves sprawled across a neighboring passenger. The writer added, however: "One poor fellow went crazy from loss of sleep; and to prevent mischief to himself and others we

(ABOVE) *Early travelers along the Gila Trail were amazed to encounter this ancient Indian high-rise structure known as Casa Grande, or Big House, which was built around A. D. 1300. Near today's Coolidge, the Casa Grande Ruins National Monument was a magnet for early tourists, and it still lures thousands today.*
JERRY JACKA

(FOLLOWING PANEL, PAGES 32 AND 33) *General Stephen Watts Kearny's 1846 encounter with friendly Indians at the Pima Villages along the Gila River southeast of today's Phoenix.*

were obliged to strap him fast in the boot [baggage compartment] and leave him at the next station."

Oatman Massacre

In 1851, tragedy overtook the family of Royse Oatman, traveling to California by wagon on the Gila Trail. Other wagons had dropped out of their train at Tucson, the Pima Villages, and Maricopa Wells. Foolishly, impatiently, the Oatman family went on alone.

Text continued on page 34

Text continued from page 31

Thirty miles beyond the bend of the Gila, they ate the last of their groceries, a supper of dry bread and bean soup. A party of Indians approached and demanded food, but Royse Oatman said he had none.

The Indians killed Oatman, his wife, and four of their seven children. They left a son, Lorenzo, for dead, and took captive daughters Olive, 12, and Mary Ann, 8. Their captors, Yavapais, soon traded the girls to Mojaves in northwestern Arizona.

Mary Ann died a year later. Olive lived as a captive of the Indians for five years, until a man at Fort Yuma learned her whereabouts and ransomed her from the Mojaves for a white horse, four blankets, some beads, and a few trinkets. She was reunited with Lorenzo, who had made his way to California. An exaggerated book about her captivity was a best-seller in 1857.

Water in the Gila

Water flowed in the Gila River then, especially downstream from where the waters of the Salt River poured in. A man from Arkansas, Alden M. Woodruff, wrote of buying melons, corn, and feed for animals at the Pima Villages, then continuing west along the Gila. "We soon learned how to find grass," he wrote. "We had to swim our stock over to the [sand] bars and islands, and on some found plenty of fine grass."

But Woodruff's two best mules injured themselves pulling their hooves from the quicksand. He traded them off for one good mule, packed what belongings that mule could carry, and abandoned his wagon.

The Gila was 150 yards wide, and perhaps four or five feet deep at its deepest point, but the water level varied from time to time. Some Forty-niners lashed logs to their wagon beds to make flatboats and floated downstream to Yuma. That didn't work out too well for the Mormon Battalion, though. Captain Cooke ordered that two wagon beds be lashed between cottonwood logs and floated toward Yuma. Lieutenant George Stoneman commanded this rude vessel. But the river was too shallow and Stoneman had to throw precious supplies overboard, along with some of Cooke's personal belongings.

Much of the Gila River is dry today, except in times of rain. Not only was it dammed far upstream, but the Salt River and its tributary Verde River also were dammed.

The Gila crosses some harsh areas of Sonoran Desert, but it is not the barren desert you see in cartoons about Death Valley. In the winter and spring, the desert is green with cactus, shrubs, and grass.

Crisp mountains always seem nearer than they are. They have changing moods: mysterious, promising, forbidding, depending on the time of day. The swift trip along the freeway makes travelers glad they didn't have to cross the desert in a covered wagon, worrying about where to find food and water for the mules or oxen.

Arizona's First Train

As the Gila approaches the Colorado River, Interstate 8 swoops through Telegraph Pass and drops into the modern farming community of Yuma. It was here that the Southern Pacific Railroad put the first train into Arizona in 1877. In fact, during our entire trip across the Gila Trail, we have paralleled the Southern Pacific mainline, and that's another important part of our story, for a couple of reasons.

While horses, mules, oxen, and even camels were penetrating the West, the steam engine

(ABOVE, RIGHT) *Travelers on the Butterfield Stage in 1858 did not ride in comfort. They bounced over desert trails in small wagons much like this one, pictured in later years at a territorial hotel.* ARIZONA HISTORICAL SOCIETY

(RIGHT) *Primitive stage stops, such as the remains of this adobe building near Filibuster Camp east of Yuma, offered few comforts.* ARIZONA HISTORICAL SOCIETY

The iron horse first came to Arizona in 1877, when the Southern Pacific Railroad pushed its tracks eastward from California to Yuma. The Colorado River was a formidable barrier to railroad construction, and later to highway building. But engineers spanned the river with mammoth bridges. ARIZONA HISTORICAL SOCIETY

was being developed in the East. Men had learned that steam, expanding in an iron cylinder, could drive a piston back and forth, powering locomotives and steamboats. The steam engine revolutionized transportation and helped build America.

The United States bought southern Arizona below the Gila River from Mexico in 1854 to acquire land for a southern railroad route across the country. That railroad didn't reach Tucson until 1880, 26 years after the Gadsden Purchase.

In the meantime, steamboats opened up another important Arizona pathway, the Colorado River. The most important river port was Yuma, where the Gila Trail entered California.

For more than 160 years, the Gila Trail has been important to the adventuresome people who came to Arizona. It has been even more important to the United States, connecting the Pacific coast to the East and helping weld a nation together. ☐

Important Dates on the Gila Trail

- 1825-26: Mountain men explore the Gila River. Those same years also see the invention of the first steam locomotive, the John Stevens.

- 1846: The Mormon Battalion joins the Gila Trail with a wagon road from the southeast. Also, the Mexican War begins.

- 1849-50: Gold-seekers use the Gila Trail to reach California. In 1849, slavery was banned in the District of Columbia.

- 1858-61: Butterfield Overland Mail travels the Gila Trail. Also, 1858 brings about the Dred Scott fugitive slave decision.

- 1877-80: Southern Pacific Railroad built from Yuma to Tucson. Woolworth's first five and dime store opens in Utica, New York, 1879.

Where the Colorado River empties into the Gulf of California, enterprising steamboat captains of the mid-19th century loaded passengers and freight onto shallow-draft river steamers and battled the current upstream to Yuma, and beyond. Port Isabel, built on the Sonora, Mexico mainland, served as the outfitting station for river traffic. Shrimp boats fish the gulf waters at top, center.
PETER KRESAN

Chapter 3

COLORADO RIVER ROUTE

In the days before air conditioning made desert summers endurable, a man and wife lived on the Arizona side of the Colorado River. One spring night, the flooding river cut a new channel around the east side of their house. Next morning, the husband went outside and surveyed the change in geography.

"Well, we live in California now," he told his wife.

"Oh, thank goodness," she said. "I couldn't stand another Arizona summer."

The Colorado River could tell some wild stories, although that tall tale might not be one of them. The river does occasionally swell and change its channel, causing Arizona and California to argue over the location of their common boundary.

The modern-day Colorado is a playground for fishermen, water-skiers, and campers. Seven dams along Arizona's borders provide water for farms and cities, or hydroelectric power, or both.

(ABOVE) *Two women and a little girl in proper Victorian dress await the sailing of the steamship* St.Valier *at Yuma. Colorado River steamers offered few luxuries, and were unbearably hot in summer.* ARIZONA HISTORICAL SOCIETY

In days gone by, the river played another important role for Arizona Territory: It was a pathway into the territory for steamboats. In the 25 years before railroads arrived, the paddle wheelers helped deliver supplies to remote mining towns and Army camps.

The most important town on the river was Yuma, where the Gila River enters the Colorado. Even before a town grew up there, it was the best place to cross the Colorado. Spanish missionaries and soldiers established a mission at the crossing in 1780, but Yuma Indians wiped out the settlement the following year. Mountain men exploring Arizona's other rivers always seemed to end up there, and both the Mexican and U.S. armies used the crossing during the Mexican War, 1846-48.

Traffic really got heavy during the California Gold Rush of 1849 when thousands of gold-seekers from the United States and Mexico crossed the Colorado at Yuma. Ferry operators fought to monopolize the business. Bandits lurked near the river to rob miners returning to Sonora or the eastern United States. So in 1850 a military post was established on the California side of the river. It became known as Fort Yuma. A town soon grew up on the Arizona side, originally named Colorado City, then Arizona City, then finally, Yuma.

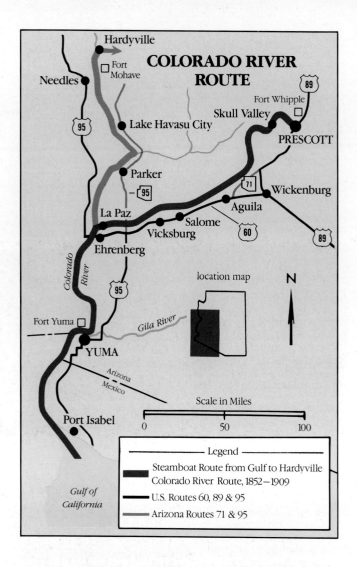

COLORADO RIVER ROUTE

location map

N

Scale in Miles
0   50   100

—— Legend ——
Steamboat Route from Gulf to Hardyville
Colorado River Route, 1852–1909
—— U.S. Routes 60, 89 & 95
—— Arizona Routes 71 & 95

Hardyville
Fort Mohave
Needles
Lake Havasu City
Skull Valley
Fort Whipple
PRESCOTT
Parker
Wickenburg
Aguila
La Paz
Salome
Vicksburg
Ehrenberg
Colorado River
Fort Yuma
Gila River
YUMA
Arizona
Mexico
Port Isabel
Gulf of California

Steamboats on the Colorado

In 1852, Captain James Turnbull of San Francisco was given a contract to supply Fort Yuma. Using parts of a harbor tugboat and a steam engine from a locomotive, he put together the crude steamer *Uncle Sam* where the Colorado River empties into the Gulf of California.

By 1864, five larger stern-wheel boats and four barges plied the Colorado. Ships from San Francisco unloaded goods more than 100 miles south of Yuma at Port Isabel, a crude port near the mouth of the river. The shallow-draft steamboats, which could operate in only a few inches of water, carried the goods upstream.

Freight delivered by the steamboats was more precious than gold to Arizona settlers. As late as 1864, miners around Arizona's new territorial capital, Prescott, had gold in their pockets, but nothing to buy. They wore tattered clothes, and many had only wild game to eat.

Provisions shipped overland by mule trains from Santa Fe or San Francisco were scarce and very expensive. Flour sold for as much as $1 a pound. Soon, however, a combination of riverboats and wagons supplied Prescott.

Some of the soldiers who manned frontier Army posts also traveled by river boat. It was hardly a pleasure cruise. Some died from the heat while waiting at Port Isabel for a steamer to take them upriver.

The river current was swift and unpredictable before dams were built, and it took 10 days or more for a steamboat to labor upstream past the low willow and mesquite covered river banks to Yuma.

The boats had to stop frequently at woodyards, where Mexican and Indian woodcutters made a living supplying fuel for the steam engines. The woodyards, one every few miles, continued more than 400 miles upriver.

A steamboat would pull in to shore and workers would carry aboard armloads of wood. A fire in a firebox heated water in a boiler. Steam from the boiler powered pistons, and they in turn moved long metal beams which turned the paddle wheel at the stern.

Yuma

Some cartoonists have drawn Arizona as the profile of a man facing California across the river. Yuma is at the top of the "chin," where the Gila River forms a "mouth." Yuma is a modern farming town, and a favorite destination for winter visitors from colder climates. The town remembers its heritage at Yuma Quartermaster Depot Park, where ferries crossed in the 1850s. Some of the civilian and Army Quartermaster Corps buildings are being restored on the old river front, where steamboats used to tie up.

Above Yuma, the Colorado River goes between banks that occasionally rise in bluffs

(LEFT) *A sophisticated system of irrigation canals brings Colorado River water to fields near Yuma, one of Arizona's most important agricultural areas.* JERRY SIEVE

(ABOVE) *Yuma Territorial Prison State Historic Park preserves the buildings and memories of Arizona's infamous 19th-century prison.* JEFF GNASS

(BELOW) *Before bridges spanned the waters of the Colorado, travelers crossed the river on the Yuma Ferry.* ARIZONA HISTORICAL SOCIETY

and stone knobs. A few miles north, Laguna Dam diverts water to farms below Yuma, and Imperial Dam sends water to the Imperial Valley of California.

Due to the extreme heat and little rainfall, western Arizona has a distinctive, barren character. Plants are sparse and jagged mountains have the stark beauty of stone outcroppings uncluttered by vegetation. Near the river there is enough water for green trees and brush, patches of farmland, and shady backwaters, but it is still hot. River towns, ranging from 141 to 675 feet above sea level, report some of the hottest summertime temperatures in the nation.

In 1874, somewhere not far north of Yuma, Army wife Martha Summerhayes described the progress of the steamboat *Gila*, captained by Jack Mellon:

Text continued on page 44

(FOLLOWING PANEL, PAGES 42 AND 43) *Colorado River steamboats were smaller and less luxurious than the boats on the Mississippi, but these agile Colorado boats could navigate in 24 inches of water and were able to come to the river's edge to receive freight.*

"Jack Mellon was then the most famous pilot on the Colorado, and he was very skillful in steering clear of the sand bars, skimming over them, or working his boat off, when once fast upon them.

"The deckhands, men of a mixed Indian and Mexican race, stood ready with long poles, in the bow, to jump overboard, when we struck a sandbar, and by dint of pushing, and reversing the engine, the boat would swing off.

"On approaching a shallow place, they would sound with their poles, and in a sing-song high-pitched tone drawl out the number of feet (to the bottom of the river). Sometimes their sleepy drawling tones would suddenly cease, and crying loudly, 'No alli agua!' (There is no water there) they would swing themselves over the side and begin their strange and intricate manipulations with the poles.

"Passengers, meanwhile, stood on deck to watch the tedious process, or sought shade in tiny, cramped cabins."

(ABOVE) *During the 1870s, freight delivered by riverboats was stored at Ehrenberg's Army quartermaster warehouse. Supplies were then loaded onto wagons for the long haul to Arizona's cavalry posts in the interior of Arizona Territory.* ARIZONA HISTORICAL SOCIETY

(RIGHT) *One of America's finest bird sanctuaries, the Imperial National Wildlife Refuge, is along the Colorado River just north of Yuma. Here white pelicans rest in shallow water near the shore.* PETER ENSENBERGER

Ehrenberg

Interstate 10 from Phoenix to Los Angeles bridges the river at Ehrenberg, the site of one of the most interesting old river ports. One of the territory's first mining booms started in 1862 at nearby La Paz. The town that sprang up there was briefly the seat of Yuma County and was proposed as the territorial capital. But floods changed the path of the Colorado, leaving La Paz a long way from the river bank.

The trade shifted to Ehrenberg. A couple of steamboat captains helped found the port, and they made sure the freight landed there.

Martha Summerhayes had expected something grander than what she saw at Ehrenberg. She wrote in 1878, "Visions of castles on the Rhine, and stories of the Middle Ages floated through my mind... Alas! for my ignorance. I saw but a row of low thatched hovels, perched on the edge of the ragged looking river-bank; a road ran lengthwise along [it], and opposite the hovels I saw a store and some more mean-looking huts of adobe."

From the dock at Ehrenberg, freight wagons hauled supplies over 160 miles of rough desert and mountain road. En route to the territorial capital in Prescott, the road gained more than a mile in elevation. As complicated as the ocean, river, and land trip was, freight could be delivered for half the rate demanded by overland teamsters.

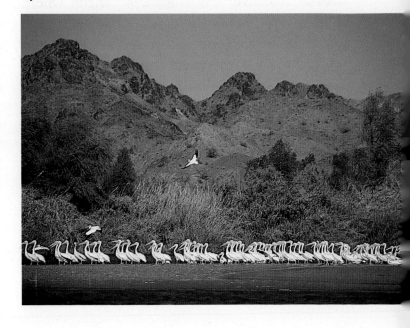

Arizona's Navy

Another bridge crosses to California at Parker, 47 miles above Ehrenberg. Upstream from Parker, the river enters a steep canyon where Parker Dam was built in the 1930s to divert water to Los Angeles. The governor of Arizona sent the National Guard to block the start of Parker Dam and prevent the loss of water Arizonans felt was theirs. There were few roads in the area then, and no bridges. Nellie Bush, the state's only woman river pilot, loaned some of her small boats to the soldiers. State officials later proclaimed her "commodore" of the fictional "Arizona Navy."

Not a shot was fired, but the picturesque military action forced the courts to decide how the waters of the Colorado River should be divided among the states. After decades of

London Bridge, which once spanned the Thames River, now straddles Colorado River waters at Lake Havasu City, one of Arizona's premier vacation and retirement communities. JERRY SIEVE

legal and legislative action, the Central Arizona Project canal now delivers water to central and southern Arizona from Lake Havasu, behind Parker Dam.

Lake Havasu City

Fifteen miles up the lake, developers created Lake Havasu City in 1963. To make the new town more interesting, they bought remnants of London Bridge. Stone blocks were shipped from England and reassembled across a channel dug for that purpose. A touristy "olde English village" was added nearby.

Twenty miles north of Lake Havasu City, In-

terstate Route 40 and the Santa Fe Railroad cross the river at Topock. Above Topock, the river passes the farms of the Fort Mohave Indian Reservation, across the river from Nevada's southern tip. It was to bleak Fort Mohave that Martha Summerhayes and her soldier husband reported in 1874, to begin their hard overland journey to Fort Apache.

Prescott's historic "Nob Hill," on East Union Street, boasts some of the West's finest Victorian homes such as the Henry Goldwater house, at left, built in 1894. JERRY JACKA

Bullhead City

Above Fort Mohave, and about 310 miles upriver from Yuma, the modern town of Bullhead City stretches along the river. Across the river, small ferries take gamblers from casino to casino in Laughlin, Nevada. An excursion boat, a replica of a river steamer, takes travelers south to Lake Havasu City.

In central Bullhead City, a small stone monument is almost hidden at the entrance to a restaurant. It reminds visitors that this was once the riverport of Hardyville. Captain William Hardy established a port here in 1864. For a brief time, much of the freight bound for Prescott went over Captain Hardy's toll road.

Hardyville was the "practical head of navigation" on the Colorado. While some steamboats struggled farther up the rugged canyons, this was as far as a boat could count on going in most years.

Railroads and Dams

Beginning in 1877, railroads gradually took over the freight business. Steamboats continued to operate for many years, however, supplying mines along the river.

Captain Mellon sold his last steamer, *Cochan*, in 1909, the year Laguna Dam blocked the river just above Yuma. The last steamboat, *Searchlight*, was wrecked in 1916.

Railroads began to serve Prescott, Arizona's territorial capital, in the 1880s. The mile-high community had what one writer called an "American" look, more familiar to Americans from the East than the more rustic frontier buildings of other towns. Victorian homes

(TOP) *By the 1890s, Prescott, Arizona Territory's first capital (1864-67), had developed into an important center of mining and commerce.* ARIZONA HISTORICAL FOUNDATION

(ABOVE) *When the railroad reached Prescott in 1887, joining the city with the outside world, the importance of the Yuma-Ehrenberg-Prescott freight route was diminished. Here workers build the railroad across the high country from Williams to Prescott.* NATIONAL ARCHIVES

from territorial days still stand along Prescott's tree-lined streets. Its old-fashioned business district surrounds a New England-style courthouse square.

Prescott, nestled in a bowl among forested mountains, is one of the favorite summer destinations of modern Arizonans, and, about 160 miles away, the Colorado River is a playground for water sports enthusiasts. Today, noisy jet ski boats and quiet fishing craft navigate waters where sweating deck hands once labored to supply the outposts of the Arizona Territory. ☐

Important Dates Along The Colorado River

• 1539: Francisco de Ulloa discovers river's mouth.

• 1775: Spanish expedition that founds San Francisco crosses the Colorado River at Yuma. The same year, Paul Revere makes his famous ride.

• 1849-50: Thousands of gold-seeking Forty-niners use the crossing. The U.S. Postal Service issues its first adhesive postage stamp.

• 1850: Fort Yuma founded. New Mexico Territory (including Arizona) is organized.

• 1852: First steamboat on the Colorado. *Uncle Tom's Cabin* is published.

• 1862: Gold discovered at La Paz. Civil War battles of Shiloh and New Orleans are fought.

• 1877: Southern Pacific Railroad enters Arizona. Rutherford B. Hayes declared president after a much-disputed election.

• 1909: Laguna Dam begins to block river transportation. Admiral Robert Peary reaches the North Pole.

The deep gorge of Canyon Diablo, south of the Little Colorado River, frustrated Edward Beale as he charted a wagon road across northern Arizona in 1857. It later caused a long delay in building the first railroad.
RICHARD WESTON

Chapter 4

BEALE'S WAGON ROAD

There is no way of knowing now which explorer was more surprised on the morning of January 23, 1858. Captain George Johnson had taken the side-wheeled *General Jesup* farther up the Colorado River than any steamboat had gone before. Soon after he started back down the river toward Yuma, Johnson put into shore near the spot where the southern tip of Nevada would later join Arizona and California.

There he found men, mules, wagons, and 23 large awkward-looking camels from the Middle East. They carried supplies for another explorer, Edward F. Beale, who was returning along the wagon road he had pioneered the previous autumn.

Johnson ferried Beale's party across the river. The explorers had connected two colorful Arizona pathways.

Perhaps camels did not seem as exotic then as they do now. Just as we try out new equipment to see if it can do a better job, the U.S. government wanted to learn if camels would be useful pack animals in the American West.

Beale, an adventuresome former Navy officer, had been assigned to establish a new wagon road to California along the 35th parallel and was just the right man to try camels. He was impressed with them and wrote in his diary: "I look forward to the day when every mail route across the continent will be conducted and worked altogether with the economical and noble brute."

Camels did not catch on, obviously. However, Beale also predicted that the route he was exploring from New Mexico to California would become "the great emigrant road to California." That prediction came true.

(ABOVE) *Historic Route 66, built in the 1920s, crossed much empty country such as this stretch west of Seligman. It also ran through hundreds of small towns earning the name "Main Street of America."* NORMAN WALLACE

(FOLLOWING PANEL, PAGES 50 AND 51) *The historic 1858 meeting of Beale's camels and Capt. George Johnson's steamboat, the* General Jesup, *on the Colorado River.*

Road of Many Names

The road has been called several things: Beale's Wagon Road, U.S. Route 66, "The Main Street Of America," and now U.S. Interstate 40. Route 66 was the subject of a popular song and a television series. Although it connected

Text continued on page 52

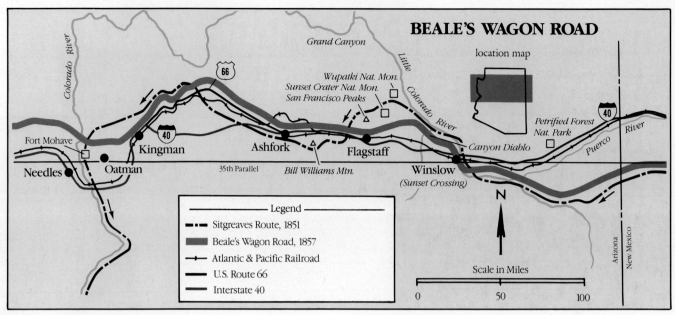

BEALE'S WAGON ROAD

location map

Legend
- Sitgreaves Route, 1851
- Beale's Wagon Road, 1857
- Atlantic & Pacific Railroad
- U.S. Route 66
- Interstate 40

Grand Canyon

Wupatki Nat. Mon.
Sunset Crater Nat. Mon.
San Francisco Peaks

Petrified Forest Nat. Park

Colorado River

Little Colorado River

Puerco River

Fort Mohave · Kingman · Ashfork · Flagstaff · Canyon Diablo

Needles · Oatman

35th Parallel · Bill Williams Mtn. · Winslow (Sunset Crossing)

Arizona / New Mexico

N

Scale in Miles
0   50   100

Text continued from 49

with other roads that together made a coast-to-coast highway, Route 66 was most famous between Chicago and Los Angeles.

The United States acquired what is now central and northern Arizona in 1848, at the end of the Mexican War, and for 15 years it was part of New Mexico Territory. The pathway had its beginning when the government sent several explorers west to find out what the new investment was all about. Each party traveled along the 35th parallel, and the leaders kept journals.

Beale described the route as colorfully as anyone. As a Navy lieutenant, he had been a hero during the war with Mexico. Then he made a daring overland trip to Washington, D.C. in 1848 to report the discovery of gold in California, and his report started the Gold Rush of 1849.

Beale began his 1857 trip in Texas, gathering a caravan of 23 camels, eight mule-drawn wagons, 350 sheep, and 56 men. At times he rode a big white dromedary (a one-humped camel) named Said (pronounced sah-eed). Other times he rode in a red ambulance (a kind of sturdy passenger wagon not necessarily meant to haul sick people). Villagers along the Rio Grande River in New Mexico thought the caravan was a traveling animal show.

On August 31, 1857, Beale's party started westward from Zuni, New Mexico, not far from where the modern freeway enters Arizona from New Mexico through the canyon of the Puerco River. Beale wrote, "The Puerco has a few cottonwood trees on its banks, and at a short distance on the hillsides, scattering cedars of stinted growth."

Soon the river emerges onto rolling plains. Beale said the terrain was "very easy everywhere for our wagons."

Today this is the southern end of the vast Navajo Indian Reservation, where an estimated 200,000 Navajos live. Explorers of the 1850s rarely saw Navajos, who at that time lived farther north.

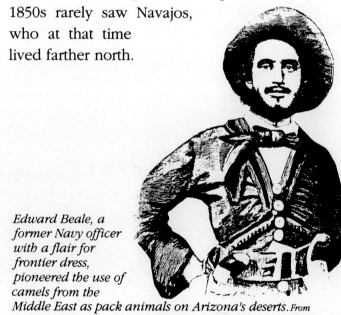

Edward Beale, a former Navy officer with a flair for frontier dress, pioneered the use of camels from the Middle East as pack animals on Arizona's deserts. From The Image of Arizona — Pictures from the Past, *by Andrew Wallace, University of New Mexico Press*

(OPPOSITE PAGE) *The San Francisco Peaks rising, as Beale described it, "apparently out of a vast plain," served as a guidepost for many an early explorer in northern Arizona.* DAVID W. LAZAROFF

Petrified Forest

Beale reported seeing petrified logs where Petrified Forest National Park is located today. Back in 1851, Lieutenant Lorenzo Sitgreaves, the first government explorer along the 35th parallel, had traveled a route which criss-crossed that of Beale. Sitgreaves wrote a more detailed description: "The ground was strewed with pebbles of agate, jasper, and chalcedony and masses of what appeared to have been stumps of trees petrified into jasper, beautifully striped with bright shades of red, blue, white, and yellow."

The north entrance to Petrified Forest National Park is just off of Interstate 40. The Painted Desert also can be seen from there. Its sand and stone formations, banded in red, orange, blue, black, brown, and gray, appear intermittently across northern Arizona.

The Puerco River flows into the Little Colorado River at the town of Holbrook. Both rivers are frequently dry, but they ran muddy streams when Beale reached the junction, as it had been raining for several days.

On September 4 he wrote, "The weather this morning is quite warm, giving us a fine chance to dry our blankets; and the men are pleased again, after cooking several days with greasewood [a low bush] to see the fine large [cottonwood] trees which grow in such abundance here."

For the next several days the explorers

(BELOW, AND OPPOSITE PAGE) *The multi-colored landscape of the Petrified Forest in northeastern Arizona has fascinated travelers since Lt. Lorenzo Sitgreaves first wrote about it in 1851. In addition to remains of ancient trees, the Petrified Forest today is yielding fossils of huge reptiles that roamed the earth even before the dinosaurs. And all of it is protected by the National Park Service and open to the public.* JERRY SIEVE/JACK DYKINGA

(CLOCKWISE FROM LEFT) *Lush summer grasses and wildflowers carpet the meadows at the base of the San Francisco Peaks. Once an active volcano, the Peaks rise to more than 12,000 feet, the highest point in Arizona.* JERRY SIEVE

Early travelers on Beale's road found ample game in the high country of northern Arizona, such as this herd of antelope grazing near Flagstaff. BLAINE D. WRIGHT

Lumbering was Flagstaff's first major industry. But it was hard work in the late 1890s felling trees by hand. NORTHERN ARIZONA PIONEER HISTORICAL SOCIETY

---

made good time across a region that Sitgreaves described best: "The surrounding scenery resembled the northwestern prairies, the country being bare of trees and the horizon unbroken."

The Little Colorado River gathers tributary streams from the mountainous Mogollon Rim country to the south. At the present-day railroad town of Winslow, the river leaves the highway route and goes northwest to join the main Colorado River at the beginning of Grand Canyon.

San Francisco Peaks

Near the site of Winslow, the explorers saw a reference point on the horizon. Beale wrote: "San Francisco Mountain, rising apparently out of a vast plain, stood as the landmark which was to be our guide for many days."

The San Francisco Peaks rise to 12,643 feet, the highest point in Arizona. These often snow-capped volcanic mountains stand purple against a sky that is usually clear and blue. They are sacred to Navajos and Hopis, and very special to many non-Indians.

Beale wrote, "We have seen indications of the greatest abundance of game...elk, antelope, and deer, besides beaver and coyotes in large numbers."

He said of the camels, "Certainly there never was anything so patient and enduring and so little troublesome as this noble animal. They pack their heavy load of corn, of which

they never taste a grain; put up with any food offered them without complaint, and are always [keeping] up with the wagons."

The camels ate whatever grass and brush was available, and carried nearly 600 pounds apiece, twice what a mule could carry, with a longer, more efficient stride.

Today, bridges carry the highway and the Santa Fe Railroad across Canyon Diablo, between Winslow and Flagstaff. Beale, however, had to go 30 miles out of his way to get around the chasm. He wrote, "This is the more annoying as the country directly across it presents to the eye an almost unbroken plain, rising very gradually to the base of the San Francisco Mountain."

On Christmas Eve, 1853, the expedition of Captain Amiel W. Whipple encountered snow where the high plain rises into the edge of a ponderosa pine forest. Whipple's men had a gala Christmas party among the trees, singing and reminiscing about their homes. Some

even set fire to a grove of pine trees, hardly an acceptable way of lighting Christmas trees.

From Wagons to 18-Wheelers

The corridor explored by Sitgreaves, Whipple, and Beale has since been used by several generations of travelers. Sleek, 18-wheel semi-trucks now roll where huge freight wagons, drawn by teams of 12 to 20 mules, once carried supplies for a new territory. The road was paved in the 1920s and '30s, when it was Route 66. Impoverished farmers traveled this way in the 1930s, after a drought turned their farmlands on the southern Great Plains into the "Dust Bowl."

Many American families go this way to California. Some travelers, crossing the plateau at

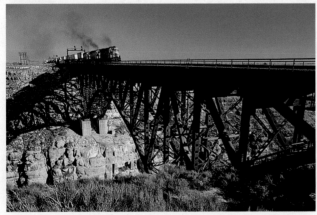

(TOP) *A volcano erupted nine centuries ago near Flagstaff, forming Sunset Crater. The lofty cinder cone, preserved as a national monument, attracts thousands of visitors each year.* JERRY SIEVE

(ABOVE) *Today the trains of the Santa Fe rumble across the Diablo Canyon bridge between Flagstaff and Winslow, as they retrace the route of Beale's Wagon Road.* RICHARD WESTON

night, are surprised at dawn when they find themselves in Flagstaff at the base of the San Francisco Peaks. The city is over 7,000 feet in elevation and surrounded by forest.

The Atlantic & Pacific Railroad, forerunner of the Santa Fe, crossed Arizona between 1880 and 1883, paralleling Beale's Road. Flagstaff was a sawmill town, supplying ties for the railroad. It took its name from an event which occurred July 4, 1876, when pioneers trimmed the limbs from a tall pine and ran up the U.S. flag. Flagstaff is still the center of a busy lumbering industry.

Four miles west of Flagstaff, the Arizona Divide separates the watersheds of the Little Colorado River and the Verde River, part of the Gila River system. Because elevations range

from 7,281 feet here to about 500 feet at the Colorado River, climate across northern Arizona can vary from bitter cold to extreme heat.

Flagstaff and Williams, 30 miles west, are gateways to the Grand Canyon, 81 miles northwest of Flagstaff. Nearly 4 million people a year visit Grand Canyon National Park.

Along Interstate 40, the forest continues a few miles west of Williams. Then the land begins dropping toward the Colorado River. The road descends 1,630 feet in the 19-mile stretch between Williams and Ash Fork, leaving the Colorado Plateau.

(TOP) *The snow-capped San Francisco Peaks, viewed from Lomakai Ruin at Wupatki National Monument northeast of Flagstaff.*

(ABOVE) *Nearby Wukoki Ruin, in the same national monument. The Sinagua and Anasazi Indians built these structures around A.D. 1065, and the National Park Service has preserved them to give today's visitors a feel for the Native Americans' way of life centuries ago.*
BOTH BY TOM DANIELSEN

Farewell to the Camel

From this point westward, Beale found the going was not as easy as it had been. The land was more jumbled, and the easiest route not so obvious to find.

Beale's report continued to praise camels. For several years after the expedition, the gov-

ernment experimented with the animals. However, others found them stubborn, noisy, and smelly. Few soldiers wanted anything to do with them, and the sight of camels stampeded horse teams.

The experiment ended when the Civil War began in 1861. After the war, railroads began to take over the job of hauling freight and mail. By 1883 the Atlantic & Pacific Railroad (which later became the Atchison, Topeka & Santa Fe) had crossed northern Arizona. The fast trains hauled people and supplies to Arizona, and carried away the gold, silver, and copper mined there, as well as cattle from the territory's ranches.

At the town of Seligman, Beale's Road and the Santa Fe Railroad veer northwest. The sec-

tion of Interstate 40 which takes a more direct route west to Kingman opened in 1978. The bypassed section of Route 66, 89 miles long between Seligman and Kingman, is the longest identifiable stretch of what was once "The Main Street of America." The Arizona Department of Transportation has designated it a historic route.

In the area between Seligman and the river, the early explorers began to encounter Indians, some of them hostile. Antoine Leroux, a mountain man who guided both Sitgreaves and Whipple, was wounded by arrows in a fight in 1851. Beale's men were prepared for a fight, but found the Indians peaceful. Beale traded with them. "In a day," he wrote, "we had secured a hundred bushels of corn and

(OPPOSITE PAGE) *In 1916, the gold and silver mining town of Oatman was booming in the mountains east of the Colorado River along Beale's road. Even in this early year automobiles had already replaced horses and wagons on the main street.* MOHAVE COUNTY HISTORICAL SOCIETY

(ABOVE) *Seven decades later, Oatman stands as a well-preserved "ghost town" catering to tourists looking for a taste of yesterday.* JAMES TALLON

beans, pumpkins, watermelons, and cantaloupes."

Like many other towns across northern Arizona, Kingman began as a railroad town, then served travelers along Route 66. It also has been a mining center.

The Colorado River, 30 miles due west of Kingman, is 2,800 feet lower than the town. Beale went straight west to the river. Later highways veered southward to find an easier path.

For a different view, let's go to 1916. Jeannie Lippitt Weeden, an early motorist from Rhode Island, wrote: "Leaving Kingman, it was the hardest day's work yet to make the 73 miles to Needles. Forty miles of bad roads with heavy sand, dry washes and wet ones, too, stones, up and down all kinds and depths of 'hollows,' some fords, until we reached Topock, Arizona. Here we crossed the bridge over the Colorado River and are in California at last."

Beale was glad to reach California, too, although he didn't find a bridge. The camels swam across the river October 18, 1857. Beale continued to his ranch in California and rested, then returned in January, 1858, to test his new road in winter.

That's when he met Captain Johnson and the steamship *General Jesup*. He reported, "It is difficult to conceive the varied emotions with which this news is received. Here, in a wild, almost unknown country, inhabited only by savages, the great river of the West had, for the first time, borne upon its bosom the emblem of civilization, a steamer."

Less than a month later, Beale finished his survey and wrote: "I have tested the value of the camels [and] marked a new road to the Pacific."

You don't see many camels today, and the steamboats are gone. Beale's road to the Pacific, however, is now a broad freeway carrying travelers over the top of Arizona. □

Important Dates Along Beale's Road

- 1848: Northern part of Arizona and New Mexico acquired from Mexico by the Treaty of Guadalupe Hidalgo. The same year gold is discovered in California.

- 1851: Sitgreaves Expedition. Melville's *Moby Dick* is published.

- 1853-54: Whipple Railroad Survey. 1853, Commodore Perry opens Japan to trade with the West.

- 1857-58: Beale's camel caravan.

- 1883: Atlantic & Pacific Railroad crossed Colorado River at Topock.

- 1926: Beale's Road designated U.S. Route 66. First liquid fuel rocket fired.

- 1978: Interstate 40 completed, except for two community bypasses. Panama Canal turned over to Panama.

Chapter 5

HONEYMOON TRAIL

William Hamblin was such a good marksman with a rifle that his companions called him "Gunlock Bill." While the men were camped at a remote spring, they started to discuss just how good he was. One thing led to another and soon they were betting Hamblin couldn't shoot the bottom out of Dudley Leavitt's pipe from 50 paces away.

Leavitt was smart enough to take the pipe out of his mouth and lay it on a rock. Gunlock Bill took careful aim and did indeed shoot the bottom out of it. Legend says that's how Pipe Spring got its name, back in 1858.

Today, Pipe Spring National Monument is an oasis in what is called the Arizona Strip. Visitors don't expect to see such a shady, intriguing place on the remote plains near the Utah border. The fortified building that frontier ranchers built still stands, and it has been restored to show how they really lived.

Pipe Spring was one of the important overnight stops on the Honeymoon Trail, a wagon road into Arizona from the north. At first it was one of several southwestern trails called "the Mormon Trail," because many who traveled it were members of the Church of Jesus Christ of Latter-day Saints, called Mormons.

It became known as the Honeymoon Trail because it is important to Mormons that their marriages be sealed in one of their temples. Before the Arizona Temple was dedicated at Mesa in 1927, Arizona Mormons made the long arduous trip to the nearest temple in St. George, Utah.

Bill Hamblin's brother, Jacob, was a legendary pathfinder who scouted new sites for Mormon colonization. Even as a young man, the adventuresome Hamblin was called "Old Jacob," not so much a sign of respect as an affectionate nickname. The respect came later. Jacob explored southward from Utah, finding several routes into Arizona. He earned the trust of Indians in the region.

Beginning in the 1870s, families began to follow Jacob Hamblin's main trail into Arizona, gradually wearing a rough wagon road into the earth of the Colorado Plateau.

(OPPOSITE PAGE) *The fort at Pipe Spring, one of the stops on the Honeymoon Trail, has been restored as a national monument and living history museum where volunteers in costumes of the late 1800s show visitors how pioneers lived.* JAMES TALLON

(ABOVE) *A reenactment of pioneer travel over this trail gives modern "pioneers" the chance to experience the beauty of the land and the excitement of traveling by covered wagon.* VAL STANNARD

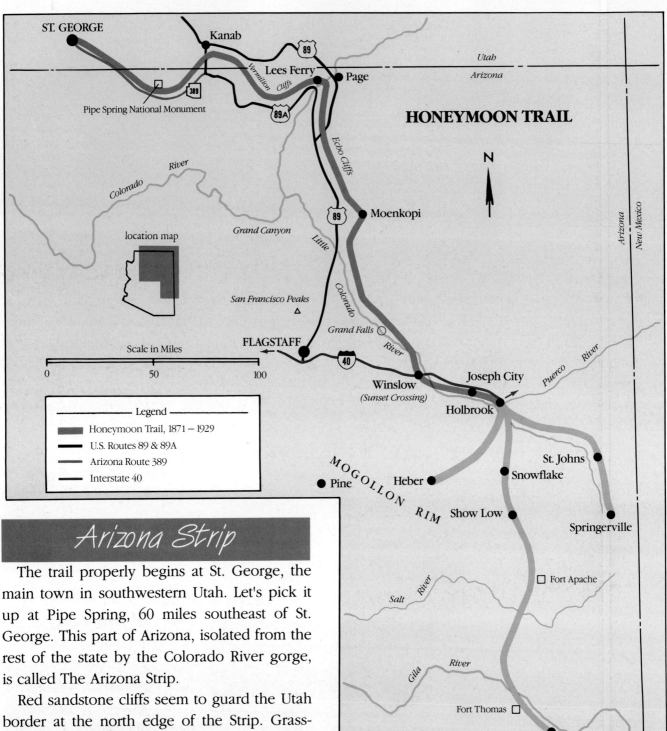

Arizona Strip

The trail properly begins at St. George, the main town in southwestern Utah. Let's pick it up at Pipe Spring, 60 miles southeast of St. George. This part of Arizona, isolated from the rest of the state by the Colorado River gorge, is called The Arizona Strip.

Red sandstone cliffs seem to guard the Utah border at the north edge of the Strip. Grasslands sweep southward from the base of the cliffs, rising gradually to a higher, timbered plateau. Its southern edge is the North Rim of Grand Canyon.

When the cattlemen settled at Pipe Spring in 1863, the grass was tall for miles around and the water from the spring was the best in the area.

The rancher and his foreman were killed by Indians, so later owners built a "fort" to protect the spring from attack by Navajo and Paiute raiders. A pair of two-story stone buildings face each other across a narrow yard, and the ends of the yard are enclosed. The structure also was called "Winsor Castle," taking the name of one of its early occupants.

Fifteen miles east of Pipe Spring on Arizona Route 389 is the little town of Fredonia. Alternate U.S. Route 89 runs north and south as Fredonia's main street. Then it bends southeast as it penetrates Arizona. For the first few miles, it lies west of the old Honeymoon Trail, but it soon takes us over part of the original route.

(ABOVE) *It was a long and arduous journey, but young Mormon couples from Arizona traveled the Honeymoon Trail to seal their marriages in the temple at St. George, Utah.* VAL STANNARD

(RIGHT) *Today a modern highway traces the route of the Honeymoon Trail along the Echo Cliffs, south of Page, Arizona.* JAMES TALLON

Kaibab Plateau

Sixteen miles southeast of Fredonia, U.S. Route 89A climbs onto the Kaibab Plateau, and into the north section of Kaibab National Forest. The highway goes from prairie at 4,680 feet to alpine forest at 7,921 feet. The North Kaibab is an ecological "island." Two subspecies of animals are found only here: the gray, tufted-eared Kaibab squirrel and the Kaibab mule deer.

The community of Jacob Lake was named for Jacob Hamblin. Here the road forks. Arizona Route 67 goes southward 45 miles to the North Rim of the Grand Canyon, while Route 89A drops off the plateau to the east, into House Rock Valley, where it again joins the original Honeymoon Trail. The valley got its name from large blocks of sandstone that pioneers used for shelter.

Before the highway reaches the valley floor, a viewpoint lets you look east toward the Vermilion Cliffs. One dictionary calls vermilion "a variable color averaging a vivid reddish orange." The cliffs do vary in colors, depending on the time of day and the weather. They look pink in dim light, bright orange at other times.

From the viewpoint, imagine a train of ox-drawn wagons moving slowly across the valley floor at the base of the cliffs. Livestock trail the wagons. People travel afoot and on horseback, wondering how far it is to the next reliable waterhole.

Caravan of Wagons

There was more grass on the Arizona Strip in the 1870s and '80s than there is now. This is one of the places where westerners learned that grass would not recover from overgrazing as rapidly as it would in wetter climates. In late summer and early fall, the rabbit brush that covers the ground bursts into golden bloom, giving color to the valley.

Some couples, returning to Utah to seal their vows, traveled north along the trail on horseback. More often, several families went in caravans of wagons so they could help each other if they ran into problems along the way.

Pioneer Arizona author Will C. Barnes traveled the Honeymoon Trail in a wagon and remembered later: "Where hills and mountains were in its way, it simply either went up and over them, or else dodged them by going miles around. When washes were running belly deep to a horse and as swift as a horse could run, the wagons went into camp and waited, sometimes days, for the water to stop running. Often, when it did stop, there were two or three feet of soft, sticky mud which necessitated hitching three or four teams of horses, aided by long ropes pulled by the men and women, to get the heavily loaded wagons through and across."

(ABOVE) *Jacob Hamblin, known as one of the great trailblazers of the west, was also a respected friend of the Navajo Indians of northern Arizona.* ARIZONA HISTORICAL SOCIETY

(OPPOSITE PAGE) *Not far from Jacob Lake (named for Jacob Hamblin) on the North Rim of the Grand Canyon is Greenland Lake, a woodland paradise often visited by mule deer.* JACK DYKINGA

Route 89A follows the wagon road east along the base of the Vermilion Cliffs. The road is gradually squeezed between the cliffs and the Colorado River, and it almost runs out of room before it reaches Lees Ferry.

Lees Ferry

The Colorado River gorge widens out at the narrow delta where the Paria River joins it from the north. Jacob Hamblin located a ferry site here in the 1860s.

Brigham Young, president of the Mormon Church, assigned John D. Lee to establish a ferry for the migration into Arizona. Lee never stayed long in one place. The United States wanted to prosecute him for his part in the Mountain Meadows Massacre in 1857, when farmers and Indians wiped out a wagon train of immigrants on their way to California. Lee was arrested in 1874 and executed in 1877.

Lee's wife, Emma, ran the ferry from the nearby farm she called Lonely Dell. The National Park Service has preserved Emma Lee's primitive log cabin, as well as other historic buildings at the crossing site.

Thousands of wagons and early automobiles crossed the river on crude ferry boats between 1871 and 1929. Now Lees Ferry is the launching spot for raft trips through Marble Canyon and the Grand Canyon. Upstream, just above the ferry, Glen Canyon, another gorge with walls of vertical stone, begins.

Fortunately, we don't have to rely on a ferry today. Four miles behind us, where we said the trail nearly ran out of room between river and cliffs, Navajo Bridge crosses Marble Canyon into "Lower Arizona." The steel arch bridge was built in 1929. It will soon be replaced by a new highway bridge, and the old bridge will serve sightseers who want to peer into the gorge at the river, 467 feet below.

For the next 80 miles, the highway closely follows the Honeymoon Trail. At Bitter Springs, Route 89A merges with Route 89 from Lake Powell.

A century and more ago, John D. Lee operated a ferry across the Colorado River, downstream from the modern Glen Canyon Dam and Lake Powell. Thousands of pioneers used Lees Ferry, as it was the only safe crossing on the Colorado for hundreds of miles.

(RIGHT) *Only the ruins of the actual ferry site remain today, but for more than four decades this place served as a major crossroads for the Southwest.* JAMES TALLON

(ABOVE) *Using irrigation methods taught to them by the pioneers, Hopi Indians farm below the village of Moenkopi, near Echo Cliffs.* JERRY JACKA

Indian Reservations

The southbound highway travels through the western end of the Navajo Indian Reservation, mentioned in the previous chapter. Here you can get a better look at the traditional Navajo way of life. Modern homes sit beside traditional hogans, wood or stone structures of six or eight sides. Navajo children tend sheep within sight of the highway. You can visit a trading post at Cedar Ridge, or The Gap.

The road parallels the Echo Cliffs, as richly colored as the Vermilion Cliffs. Gnarled juniper trees grow in some areas, but much of the land is prairie or high desert. A 10-mile detour east on U.S. Route 160 takes you to the Hopi Indian village of Moenkopi, where the Mormon pioneers taught the Hopi farmers irrigation methods still in use today.

Just before Route 89 crosses the gorge of the Little Colorado River at Cameron, it passes through another section of Painted Desert. The banded sands in this area are blue, brown, and dove gray.

The Honeymoon trail turned southeast here, following the north side of the Little Colorado about 50 miles to Grand Falls. We cannot follow that trail directly today; Route 89 continues on to Flagstaff.

Grand Falls is a series of sandstone ledges taller than Niagara Falls. In the spring, and sometimes after summer rains, a rush of muddy water cascades over the falls. More importantly to early travelers, it was the first place to avoid the river chasm. Before the Little Colorado plunges into its canyon at Grand Falls, it is a broad, flat wash, easy to cross.

The breathtaking view from the Mogollon Rim looks today much as it did 125 years ago. JERRY SIEVE

Settling Eastern Arizona

Forty miles upstream (southeast of the falls), early settlers established Sunset Crossing, near present-day Winslow. From Grand Falls or Sunset, settlers fanned out on a number of dif-

Early settlers drove their wagons down the steep face of the Mogollon Rim to make their homes near Pine and Strawberry. Because the trail plunged so steeply off the Rim, pioneers tied heavy logs to the back of their wagons to keep them from overrunning the horses.

JAMES TALLON

JAMES TALLON

Bill Ahrendt

ferent trails. Brigham Young's son, John W. Young, established an outpost in 1877 at Fort Valley, northwest of Flagstaff.

Those who settled in other parts of Arizona still faced some hard traveling. In 1879, Alfred and Ruth Randall and their five children prepared to descend the nearly vertical Mogollon Rim, 70 miles south of Grand Falls.

Ruth, who was expecting another child, sat on a rock while Alfred tied logs behind the wagons to hold them back. He didn't want the wagons to overrun the horses as they went down the steep rim. Suddenly, Ruth began to cry. Her son Fred, 11, put his arm around her and asked, "What's the matter, Ma?"

"Son, it just looks like your Pa is dragging us down to hell."

Their actual destination was the little town of Pine, where they were among the first settlers. It is a favorite summertime tourist stop for Arizonans today.

Pioneers from the Honeymoon Trail also traveled along the Little Colorado River, establishing several villages immediately east of Sunset Crossing. The only one that survives today is tiny Joseph City, between Winslow and Holbrook on Interstate Route 40. Continuing upstream (southeast), they settled at St. Johns, where there already was a community of Hispanics from New Mexico. St. Johns is the seat of Apache County. Thirty miles south of St. Johns, they founded the hamlets that became the modern towns of Springerville and Eagar, adjoining communities in Round Valley. These ranching and lumbering towns are a supply point for Arizonans who like to vacation in the White Mountains, one of Arizona's prettiest forest areas. Other areas that spun off the Honeymoon Trail include:

•Snowflake: In 1878 Erastus Snow, in charge of colonization on the Little Colorado, directed William J. Flake to buy land on Silver Creek and start a community. Their two surnames were combined to form the town's quaint name.

•Mesa: The largest satellite city of Phoenix, Mesa has more than 260,000 residents. It includes an area known as Lehi, settled in 1877.

•St. David: In 1877, those who didn't like living at Lehi settled the village of St. David in Cochise County.

•The Gila Valley: The Gila River serves a narrow band of fertile farmland through this long valley in eastern Arizona. Immigrants from Utah settled at Pima in 1879, and at Thatcher a couple of years later.

•Alpine: Southeast from Springerville, Arizona's highest year-round community is at 8,030 feet. From there the trail went on to villages in New Mexico.

"Old Jacob" Hamblin spent his final years in this area. He died at Pleasanton, New Mexico, in 1886, when he was 67, and was buried at Alpine. Hamblin's bold spirit gave us the Honeymoon Trail, one of the most colorful pathways into Arizona.□

Important Dates On The Honeymoon Trail

• 1858: Jacob Hamblin's first explorations south of the Colorado River into Arizona. First commercial oil well begins operation in Pennsylvania.

• 1871: John D. Lee established Lees Ferry. The great Chicago fire destroys most of that city.

• 1873: First large groups of immigrants used the trail to reach the Little Colorado River. First U.S. post card issued.

• 1929: Navajo Bridge replaced Lees Ferry on the road from Arizona to Utah. Stock market crash ushers in the Great Depression.

Chapter 6

ARIZONA TODAY

Pioneers used our five pathways to transform a raw territory into a modern state which now has one of the fastest rates of population growth in the United States.

While Arizona ranks as the sixth most spacious state in the nation, it also is considered one of the most "urban," with 80 percent of the population living in cities and towns. The most populous part of Arizona, the Phoenix metropolitan area, was not on any of the early pathways. Yet more than half of the state's four million residents live there today.

How did that happen? The story began centuries before the major trails were explored by people of European descent. We mentioned the Pima Villages, where generations of pioneers bought supplies for the journey west along the Gila Trail. The Pimas are believed to be descended from the prehistoric Hohokam people who "vanished" in the 1400s.

The Hohokam built a network of canals along the Salt and Gila rivers, and some of them lived where Phoenix is today. The city straddles the Salt River, just before the Salt joins the Gila.

Irrigating the Desert Garden

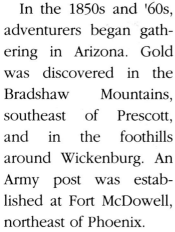

In the 1850s and '60s, adventurers began gathering in Arizona. Gold was discovered in the Bradshaw Mountains, southeast of Prescott, and in the foothills around Wickenburg. An Army post was established at Fort McDowell, northeast of Phoenix.

Farms were needed to feed miners, settlers, soldiers, and their animals. In 1867, Jack Swilling organized a company to clear out old Hohokam ditches and build new ones. The ditches took water from the Salt River to new farmland. A community began to grow along Swilling's ditch, and the downtown Phoenix townsite was laid out a little to the west of Swilling's farm in 1870.

Mild winters and early spring gave Arizona farmers a long growing season. Even today, they can send vegetable crops to market when farmers elsewhere are just beginning to plant.

(OPPOSITE PAGE) *This giant pumping station lifts precious water from Lake Havasu into the Central Arizona Project canal system, which carries water to both the Phoenix and Tucson metropolitan areas.* DON STEVENSON

(ABOVE) *Since the Hohokam Indians began irrigating their crops nearly 2,000 years ago, canals have been the life-giving arteries of Arizona.* JERRY SIEVE

It is no exaggeration to say that in most of Arizona there is always too little water, or too much. Drought is interrupted by occasional devastating floods. Farmers in the Salt River Valley wanted to store more water, and control floods. In a canyon 60 miles northeast of Phoenix, they found a site to build Theodore Roosevelt Dam, completed in 1911. A network of major canals fed the system of ditches. Since then, other dams have been built along the Salt and Verde rivers.

Meanwhile, railroads had connected Phoenix to the Southern Pacific across southern Arizona, and the Santa Fe mainline along Beale's Wagon Road in the north. Now farmers could easily market their crops.

Phoenix became the capital of Arizona in 1889 and was soon the largest city in the state. Other towns grew up nearby, and a metropolis began to form.

Summers were almost unbearably hot in the Salt River Valley. Before refrigeration, people lived outdoors away from the hot buildings as much as they could in the summertime.

Arizona's desert winters, however, were pleasant compared to ice and snow in other parts of the nation. And in the 1930s, evaporative coolers began to make summer living easier.

Arizona's Phenomenal Growth

During World War II, dozens of military training bases were built in Arizona, and people who trained there got a taste of Arizona living. Many of them came back after the war ended in 1945. The entire state boomed. Tucson now has an estimated 600,000 residents in its metropolitan area, the second largest in Arizona. Other urban centers are Yuma, with a population of 51,000; Flagstaff, 43,000; Sierra Vista, 36,000, and Prescott, 31,000 when its suburbs are counted.

Arizona is still an outdoors kind of place. The wide open spaces appeal not only to residents, but to visitors from all over the world. Say "Arizona," and people know it's interesting. Maybe it was a western movie they saw, or color photographs in *Arizona Highways* magazine, or a resort advertisement. Perhaps it was just a weather report.

Probably the most famous Arizona attraction, besides the weather, is Grand Canyon National Park. Because the Colorado River dug the Canyon through the Colorado Plateau, some people think it's in the state of Colorado. Most of them eventually find it in northern Arizona.

The National Park Service has more than 20 other scenic, historical, and recreational attractions in Arizona. The state also has six national forests and 29 state parks.

Many pioneers came here to look for gold or silver, to ranch or to farm. Later on, boosters bragged of the "five Cs," cattle, citrus, climate, copper, and cotton, that were important to Arizona's economy for so many years.

Climate is most important now, because it helps attract more visitors than ever before. The other four Cs are still important, but no one of them provides as many jobs as tourism, manufacturing, or construction.

The adventurer who moves to Arizona today may build computers, work in a resort, or earn his living building homes for all the other people who are moving here. Freedom is another important reason for moving to Arizona. The state has always attracted people who wanted to try a new way of living, away from old habits and customs.

Today, people come to Arizona along the Interstate highways or by jet airplane. But not too long ago, our five Arizona pathways opened the way for adventurers looking for a new life in the West. □

(TOP) *Massive cranes reach for the evening sky at the end of another day of construction. Arizona is one of the fastest growing states in the country, with thousands of people moving there each year.*

(LEFT) *Warm climate and a relaxed outdoors lifestyle make Arizona popular for tourists and residents alike. The state boasts more than 200 golf courses such as this one in Scottsdale.* BOTH BY JERRY SIEVE

(ABOVE) *Once the desert reigned supreme in the sunset's glow north of Phoenix, but today city lights show a major American metropolis thriving and expanding.* JERRY SIEVE

(INSET) *Heritage Square, with its restored turn-of-the-century houses, preserves a bit of early Arizona amid the skyscrapers of downtown Phoenix.* AL PAYNE

INDEX

Pages that are in **boldface** denote pictures. Pages followed by an "m" denotes map.

Prehistoric petroglyphs along the Gila Trail west of Maricopa.

PETER ENSENGERGER

Sunset silhouettes saguaro cactus on the "Forty-mile Desert" along the Gila Trail. WESLEY HOLDEN